It's attractions range from medieval buildings to award winning modern architecture, open spaces to world renowned museums. The Colleges, Museums and the river Cam provide interest and relaxation for students and visitors alike.

www.visitcambridge.org

CAMBRIDGE

A Little Souvenir

CHRIS ANDREWS PUBLICATIONS

Rooftops from great St Mary's Church

CAMBRIDGE

The city of Cambridge is an old English university town and the administrative centre of the county of Cambridgeshire. It lies approximately 50 miles (80 km) north-northeast of London and is surrounded by a number of smaller towns and villages. It is also at the heart of the high-technology centre known as 'Silicon Fen'. Cambridge is best known for the University of Cambridge, which includes 31 Colleges as well as the renowned Addenbrooke's Hospital, the Cavendish Laboratory, King's College Chapel, and the Cambridge University Library. The Cambridge skyline is dominated by the last two, along with the chimney of Addenbrooke's Hospital in the far south of the city and St John's College Chapel tower in the north.

The early history of the University started in 1209, when students escaping from hostile townspeople in Oxford fled to Cambridge and formed an establishment there. The oldest college that still exists, Peterhouse, was founded in 1284. One of the most impressive buildings in Cambridge, King's College Chapel, was begun in 1446 by King Henry VI and the project was completed in 1515 during the reign of King Henry VIII. Many of the Colleges were built in the

6 Punting

Medieval and Tudor times, between 1326 and 1596, followed by an expansion in the 1800's and the 20th Century, with the most recent, Robinson College 1979.

Cambridge Architecture is a fine representation of many periods and styles with the work of noted architects and designers such as Christopher Wren, William Morris, James Gibbs, Giles Gilbert Scott and many talented University members.

Cambridge University Press originated with a printing licence issued in 1534. Hobson's Conduit, the first project to bring clean drinking water to the town centre, was built in 1610 (by the Hobson of Hobson's choice), parts of which survive today.

Gardens at Magdalene College

The Town Market

Addenbrooke's Hospital was founded in 1766, the railway and station were built in 1845. According to legend, the University dictated the location of the latter, well away from the centre of town, so that the possibility of quick access to London would not distract students from their work - however there seems little basis for this in fact.

Despite having a University, Cambridge was not granted its city charter until 1951, it does not have a cathedral, which was traditionally a pre-requisite for city status. Today the University has been joined by Anglia Ruskin University, and the educational reputation has led to other bodies (such as the Open University in East

10 Trinity College fountain

Anglia) basing themselves in the city.

The University of Cambridge consists of over 100 departments, faculties and schools plus a central administration, it also has a large number of museums that are open to the public. Even if you have never visited Cambridge, it has still touched your life as the place that inspired Darwin, Newton, AA Milne, Wordsworth, John Cleese, and Stephen Hawking to name but a few. Today it is inspiring thousands of Cambridge students and leads the way in new and emerging technology as well as being a compact architectural delight and a city of enduring charm.

12 The organ in Jesus College Chapel

New Hall (now Murray Edwards College)

St Catharine's College   13

14   Christ's College (1505)

Christ's College garden   15

16 Corpus Christi College (1352)

Open day in Emmanuel College (1584)   17

18   Arcading in Emmanuel and the sundial in Downing College (1800)

Downing College 19

20   Pembroke College (1347)

22   Peterhouse College (1284, the oldest Cambridge foundation)

The Cam at night

26 Town streets are often named after the colleges they house

The Mitre and The Round Church, two of the city's distinctive buildings   27

28   St Catharine's College (1473)

Mathematical Bridge and Queens' College 29

30 Queens' College (1448)

32   King's College, (1441) the Chapel, King's Parade screen and gatehouse

The Chapel entrance 33

34 Gibbs' Building

36   Punting – that great, leisurely, Cambridge attraction

Punters vary in ability and probably in some cases, the time they stay dry...   37

38 The river at night

40 Rooftops and Gonville and Caius College

Gonville and Caius (1348)　41

42   King Henry VIII's statue above the Great Gate, Trinity College

Trinity College (1546), Porters discussion in the Great Court   43

44   Trinity College Fountain in The Great Court

St John's College, (1511) Main Gate

46   Detail over gateway in St John's College

48 Clare College and Bridge with The River Cam

50   Magdalene College (1428), arms on the outer face of First Court

Magdalene College Chapel   51

52   First Court looking to the Main Gate

The Pepys Library, Magdalene College   53

54   Jesus College, (1496) the entrance to Chapel Court

Ceiling of Jesus College Chapel

58   Sidney Sussex College (1596)

The place where all is known!

60 Robinson College (1979)

New Hall (1954) - now Murray Edwards College   61

62   Interesting shapes in Churchill College (1960)

Fitzwilliam College (1869) 63

First published 2007 by Chris Andrews Publications Ltd.

Reprinted 2009, 2011

15 Curtis Yard, North Hinksey Lane, Oxford, OX2 0LX

Telephone: +44(0)1865 723404 **www.cap-ox.com**

Photos: Chris Andrews. © Chris Andrews Publications Ltd

Grateful thanks to Visitcambridge for help, advice and material, to Richard Osmond for editorial assistance and to
Ryder and Amies (www.ryderamies.co.uk) for the image of scarves on the back cover and for all support.

ISBN 978–1905385–67-6

Front Cover: Punting on The Cam and King's College   Title page: Entrance to King's College   Back cover: College scarves